D1631915

YOU'RE GOING TO BE OKAY

summersdale

TO................................

FROM.............................

There's always tomorrow and it always gets better.

Ariana Grande

NOT EVERYTHING
THAT IS FACED CAN
BE CHANGED; BUT
NOTHING CAN BE
CHANGED UNTIL
IT IS FACED.

JAMES BALDWIN

THIS IS JUST A CHAPTER. IT'S NOT YOUR WHOLE STORY.

S. C. LOURIE

WE'RE
IN THIS
TOGETHER

**BEING KIND IS
JUST BEING OPEN
TO A POSSIBILITY
OF MAKING A SIMPLE
CHOICE THAT MAKES
A DAY A LITTLE
BIT BETTER.**

TOM HANKS

KEEP YOUR FACE
TO THE SUNSHINE
AND YOU CANNOT
SEE THE SHADOW.

HELEN KELLER

START
SMALL

Of all the liars in the world, sometimes the worst are our own fears.

Rudyard Kipling

I may not
have gone
where I
intended to
go, but I think
I have ended
up where I
needed to be.

Douglas Adams

CARING FOR
MYSELF IS NOT
SELF-INDULGENCE.
IT IS SELF-
PRESERVATION.

AUDRE LORDE

IF WE
BELIEVE THAT
TOMORROW
WILL BE
BETTER, WE
CAN BEAR
A HARDSHIP
TODAY.

Thích Nhất Hạnh

BRIGHTER DAYS ARE ON THE HORIZON

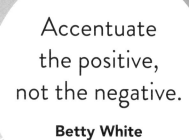

Accentuate
the positive,
not the negative.

Betty White

WHEN YOU CAN
AND AS YOU CAN,
IN WAYS THAT FEEL
LOVING, MAKE TIME
AND SPACE FOR
YOURSELF.

Tracee Ellis Ross

WE'RE
BETTER
TOGETHER

DON'T
BE AFRAID –
IF YOU ARE
AFRAID YOU
CAN'T MOVE
FORWARD.

Malala Yousafzai

THE BEST GIFT ANYONE CAN GIVE, I BELIEVE, IS THE GIFT OF SHARING THEMSELVES.

Oprah Winfrey

**Life can only
be understood
backwards;
but it must be
lived forwards.**

Søren Kierkegaard

The great gift of human beings is that we have the power of empathy, we can all sense a mysterious connection to each other.

Meryl Streep

BEST FRIENDS
MAKE GOOD
TIMES BETTER
AND HARD
TIMES EASIER

YOU'RE
GOING TO BE
OK. BETTER
THAN OK.
YOU'RE GOING
TO BE GREAT.

Reese Witherspoon

LOVE WILL FIND
A WAY THROUGH
PATHS WHERE
WOLVES FEAR
TO PREY.

LORD BYRON

I am prepared for the worst, but hope for the best.

Benjamin Disraeli

**STAY CLOSE
TO ANYTHING THAT
MAKES YOU GLAD
YOU ARE ALIVE.**

HAFEZ

YOU ARE
LOVED

LAUGHTER IS POISON TO FEAR.

GEORGE R. R. MARTIN

ONE OF THE SECRETS
OF A HAPPY LIFE IS
CONTINUOUS SMALL
TREATS, AND IF SOME
OF THESE CAN BE
INEXPENSIVE AND
QUICKLY PROCURED SO
MUCH THE BETTER.

IRIS MURDOCH

STAY
STRONG

Nothing in life is to be feared, it is only to be understood. Now is the time to understand more, so that we may fear less.

Marie Curie

UNDERSTAND
WHO YOU ARE.
EDUCATE YOURSELF
ON THE SELF.

JENNIFER ANISTON

DON'T
TRIP OVER
WHAT'S
BEHIND
YOU

WE MUST
ACCEPT FINITE
DISAPPOINTMENT,
BUT NEVER LOSE
INFINITE HOPE.

MARTIN LUTHER KING JR

LOVE YOURSELF FIRST AND EVERYTHING ELSE FALLS INTO LINE.

LUCILLE BALL

I'm no longer accepting the things I cannot change. I'm changing the things I cannot accept.

Angela Davis

SOME
PEOPLE GO
TO PRIESTS;
OTHERS TO
POETRY; I TO
MY FRIENDS.

Virginia Woolf

CELEBRATE THE SMALL THINGS

Be healthy and
take care of yourself,
but be happy with
the beautiful things
that make you, you.

Beyoncé

I LEARNED THAT COURAGE WAS NOT THE ABSENCE OF FEAR, BUT THE TRIUMPH OVER IT.

Nelson Mandela

YOU
HAVE
ALWAYS
BEEN
ENOUGH

STORMS MAKE
TREES TAKE
DEEPER ROOTS.

Dolly Parton

WE NEED
TO SIT, BE
KIND TO
OURSELVES,
AND JUST
LOOK INSIDE
FOR A
MINUTE.

Michaela Coel

You're always with yourself, so you might as well enjoy the company.

Diane von Fürstenberg

Hope is the thing
with feathers
That perches
in the soul,
And sings the tune
without the words,
And never
stops at all.

Emily Dickinson

JUST
BREATHE

IT'S ABOUT
PUTTING ONE
STEP IN FRONT
OF ANOTHER,
ABOUT FORWARD
MOVEMENT TO
WHERE YOU
WANNA BE.

Ava DuVernay

CHOOSE
HOPE AND
ANYTHING
BECOMES
POSSIBLE

Am I good enough? Yes I am.

Michelle Obama

**TRUE FRIENDS
ARE ALWAYS
TOGETHER
IN SPIRIT.**

L. M. MONTGOMERY

FOLLOWING THE BEND IN THE RIVER AND STAYING ON YOUR OWN PATH MEANS THAT YOU ARE ON THE RIGHT TRACK.

Eartha Kitt

LISTENING IS
WHERE LOVE BEGINS:
LISTENING TO
OURSELVES AND
THEN TO OUR
NEIGHBOURS.

FRED ROGERS

DON'T JUDGE EACH DAY BY THE HARVEST YOU REAP BUT BY THE SEEDS THAT YOU PLANT.

ROBERT LOUIS STEVENSON

OWNING
UP TO YOUR
VULNERABILITIES
IS A FORM OF
STRENGTH.

LIZZO

**REMEMBER THIS,
WHOEVER YOU ARE,
HOWEVER YOU ARE,
YOU ARE EQUALLY VALID,
EQUALLY JUSTIFIED,
AND EQUALLY
BEAUTIFUL.**

JUNO DAWSON

HAPPINESS BLOOMS FROM WITHIN

NOTHING IS ABSOLUTE.
EVERYTHING CHANGES,
EVERYTHING MOVES,
EVERYTHING
REVOLVES,
EVERYTHING FLIES
AND GOES AWAY.

FRIDA KAHLO

RESPECT
YOUR EFFORTS,
RESPECT
YOURSELF.

CLINT EASTWOOD

REMEMBER,
HOPE IS A GOOD THING,
MAYBE THE BEST OF
THINGS, AND NO GOOD
THING EVER DIES.

STEPHEN KING

YOU ARE YOUR BEST THING.

Toni Morrison

EVERY ONE
OF US NEEDS
TO SHOW HOW
MUCH WE
CARE FOR EACH
OTHER AND, IN
THE PROCESS,
CARE FOR
OURSELVES.

Diana, Princess of Wales

NEVER LET
A STUMBLE
IN THE
ROAD BE
THE END
OF THE
JOURNEY

You are never too small to make a difference.

Greta Thunberg

MAKING YOURSELF HAPPY IS MOST IMPORTANT. NEVER BE ASHAMED OF HOW YOU FEEL.

Demi Lovato

PROGRESS
NOT
PERFECTION

TO LEARN WHICH
QUESTIONS ARE
UNANSWERABLE,
AND NOT TO ANSWER
THEM: THIS SKILL IS
MOST NEEDFUL IN
TIMES OF STRESS
AND DARKNESS.

Ursula K. Le Guin

YOUR
FEELINGS
ARE
VALIDATED
BY THE FACT
THAT YOU'RE
FEELING
THEM.

Lili Reinhart

Without those moments where you feel like your lowest, it's impossible to appreciate the high ones.

Zac Efron

There is always something left to love.

Gabriel García Márquez

GIVING UP DOESN'T ALWAYS MEAN YOU'RE WEAK. SOMETIMES YOU'RE JUST STRONG ENOUGH TO LET GO.

TAYLOR SWIFT

LOOK FOR
THE STARS
IN THE
DARKNESS

BEGINNINGS ARE ALWAYS HARD.

Julie Andrews

Don't look too far into the future, just look at tomorrow. One day at a time.

Joe Wicks

YOU CAN'T
POUR FROM
AN EMPTY CUP

WITHOUT A STRUGGLE, THERE CAN BE NO PROGRESS.

FREDERICK DOUGLASS

START EACH DAY WITH A GRATEFUL HEART

**EVERY STRUGGLE
IN YOUR LIFE HAS
SHAPED YOU INTO
THE PERSON YOU
ARE TODAY.**

KEANU REEVES

BE GENTLE WITH
YOURSELF AND
REMEMBER THERE'S
NO ONE WAY UP
THAT MOUNTAIN.

JONATHAN VAN NESS

NOTHING CHANGES IF NOTHING CHANGES

BELIEVE IN THE GOODWILL OF PEOPLE, THE POWER OF PEOPLE TO DO SOMETHING POSITIVE.

Eddie Izzard

We're capable of so much more than we allow ourselves to believe.

Queen Latifah

IN JOINED
HANDS THERE IS
STILL SOME TOKEN
OF HOPE, IN
THE CLENCHED
FIST NONE.

VICTOR HUGO

IMAGINE WHAT COULD HAPPEN IF YOU DON'T GIVE UP

I KNOW THAT YOU CANNOT LIVE ON HOPE ALONE, BUT WITHOUT IT, LIFE IS NOT WORTH LIVING.

HARVEY MILK

COLLECT BEAUTIFUL MOMENTS

WHATEVER
IT IS YOU'RE
SEEKING WON'T
COME IN THE
FORM YOU'RE
EXPECTING.

Haruki Murakami

I am the sole
author of the
dictionary that
defines me.

Zadie Smith

REAL CHANGE, ENDURING CHANGE, HAPPENS ONE STEP AT A TIME.

Ruth Bader Ginsburg

INHALE COURAGE, EXHALE FEAR

THE FIRST STEP IS
YOU HAVE TO SAY
THAT YOU CAN.

Will Smith

STRUGGLE AND PAIN IS REAL. WE'VE ALL BEEN THERE ON SOME LEVEL OR ANOTHER.

Dwayne Johnson

Experience is never limited, and it is never complete.

Henry James

Happiness is not something I need to achieve. It's more about learning to embrace the simple truth that I am happiness.

Shailene Woodley

KEEP
GOING

THERE ARE ALWAYS GOING TO BE BAD THINGS. BUT YOU CAN WRITE IT DOWN AND MAKE A SONG OUT OF IT.

Billie Eilish

BE LOYAL
TO YOUR
FUTURE,
NOT YOUR
PAST

YESTERDAY IS HEAVY. PUT IT DOWN.

WE DO NOT GROW
ABSOLUTELY,
CHRONOLOGICALLY.
WE GROW SOMETIMES
IN ONE DIMENSION,
AND NOT IN ANOTHER;
UNEVENLY.

ANAÏS NIN

SOMETIMES SHOWING UP IS ENOUGH

THE PAIN OF
PARTING
IS NOTHING TO
THE JOY OF
MEETING AGAIN.

CHARLES DICKENS

**YOU JUST HAVE TO
GO BACK TO THAT
GREATNESS, FIND
THAT ONE LITTLE
LIGHT THAT'S LEFT.**

LADY GAGA

HAPPINESS IS
PRETTY SIMPLE:
SOMEONE TO LOVE,
SOMETHING TO DO,
SOMETHING TO
LOOK FORWARD TO.

RITA MAE BROWN

What lies behind us and what lies before us are tiny matters compared to what lies within us.

Ralph Waldo Emerson

THE BEST WAY OUT IS ALWAYS THROUGH.

ROBERT FROST

Growth is an erratic forward movement: two steps forward, one step back. Remember that and be very gentle with yourself.

Julia Cameron

ALL WE HAVE
TO DECIDE IS WHAT
TO DO WITH THE TIME
THAT IS GIVEN US.

J. R. R. TOLKIEN

TO BE HAPPY
YOU MUST BE
YOUR OWN
SUNSHINE.

CHARLES EDWARD JERNINGHAM

ACT LIKE THE PERSON YOU WANT TO BECOME

IF ONE WANTS
TO BE ACTIVE,
ONE MUST NOT
BE AFRAID OF
GOING WRONG,
ONE MUST NOT
BE AFRAID
OF MAKING
MISTAKES NOW
AND THEN.

Vincent van Gogh

THIS STORM WILL PASS

Truth has
no path. Truth is
living and, therefore,
changing.

Bruce Lee

I'M NOT CRAZY ABOUT REALITY, BUT IT'S STILL THE ONLY PLACE TO GET A DECENT MEAL.

Groucho Marx

DON'T LET ANYONE DULL YOUR SPARKLE

WITHOUT COURAGE,
WE CANNOT PRACTICE
ANY OTHER VIRTUE
WITH CONSISTENCY.
WE CAN'T BE KIND,
TRUE, MERCIFUL,
GENEROUS, OR
HONEST.

Maya Angelou

I DO NOT CARE SO MUCH WHAT I AM TO OTHERS AS I CARE WHAT I AM TO MYSELF.

Michel de Montaigne

You just have to
trust that people
are out there
waiting to love you
and celebrate you
for who you are.

Wentworth Miller

Optimism means better than reality; pessimism means worse than reality. I'm a realist.

Margaret Atwood

SEIZE THE MOMENTS OF HAPPINESS, LOVE AND BE LOVED! THAT IS THE ONLY REALITY IN THE WORLD, ALL ELSE IS FOLLY.

THERE IS NO
SMOOTH ROAD
INTO THE FUTURE:
BUT WE GO ROUND,
OR SCRAMBLE OVER
THE OBSTACLES.

D. H. Lawrence

DISTANCE MEANS SO LITTLE, WHEN SOMEONE MEANS SO MUCH

Trust yourself and trust your choices.

Denzel Washington

JUST REMEMBER,
YOU CAN DO
ANYTHING YOU SET
YOUR MIND TO,
BUT IT TAKES ACTION,
PERSEVERANCE,
AND FACING
YOUR FEARS.

GILLIAN ANDERSON

EVERY DAY IS A DAY YOU'VE NEVER SEEN BEFORE

THE HAPPIEST
PEOPLE ARE
THE PEOPLE WITH
THE BEST ATTITUDES,
NOT THE BEST
LIVES.

BOB LONSBERRY

THERE'S A POINT WHEN YOU GO WITH WHAT YOU'VE GOT. OR YOU DON'T GO.

JOAN DIDION

HOPE IS BEING
ABLE TO SEE THAT
THERE IS LIGHT
DESPITE ALL OF
THE DARKNESS.

DESMOND TUTU

HOPE IS ALWAYS STRONGER THAN FEAR

IN A TIME OF
DESTRUCTION,
CREATE SOMETHING.

MAXINE HONG KINGSTON

Power will accomplish much, but perseverance more.

William Scott Downey

YOU'VE
GOT THIS

LOOK OUT FOR YOUR SOUL

THE TRUTH IS,
NO MATTER HOW
LONELY YOU MIGHT
FEEL, YOU'RE NEVER
GOING THROUGH
ANYTHING ALONE.

JENNIFER LOPEZ

WHEN WE
STRIVE TO
BECOME
BETTER
THAN WE ARE,
EVERYTHING
AROUND US
BECOMES
BETTER.

Paulo Coelho

LIFE IS TOUGH BUT SO ARE YOU

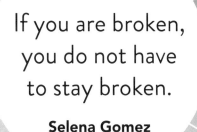

If you are broken,
you do not have
to stay broken.

Selena Gomez

THE PAST IS GONE.
TODAY IS FULL
OF POSSIBILITIES.

Karen Casey

DO IT

FOR

YOU

HOWEVER DIFFICULT
LIFE MAY SEEM,
THERE IS ALWAYS
SOMETHING YOU
CAN DO AND
SUCCEED AT.

Stephen Hawking

YOU MAKE
A LIFE OUT
OF WHAT
YOU HAVE,
NOT WHAT
YOU'RE
MISSING.

Kate Morton

I've failed over and over and over again in my life and that is why I succeed.

Michael Jordan

If we treated ourselves the way we treated our best friend, can you imagine how much better off we would be?

Meghan, Duchess of Sussex

THE UNIVERSE IS NOT OUTSIDE OF YOU. LOOK INSIDE YOURSELF; EVERYTHING THAT YOU WANT, YOU ALREADY ARE.

RUMI

HAPPINESS IS
NOT SOMETHING
READY-MADE.
IT COMES FROM
YOUR OWN
ACTIONS.

Dalai Lama

PERMISSION TO UNPLUG AND REGROUP

Nurturing one's spirit is as important as nurturing one's body and mind.

Laurence Fishburne

THE MOST IMPORTANT THING IS TO ENJOY YOUR LIFE – TO BE HAPPY – IT'S ALL THAT MATTERS.

AUDREY HEPBURN

FORGIVE
YOURSELF

CHANGE TAKES COURAGE.

ALEXANDRIA OCASIO-CORTEZ

YOUR LIFE DOES NOT GET BETTER BY CHANCE, IT GETS BETTER BY CHANGE.

JIM ROHN

DO THE HARDEST
THING ON EARTH
FOR YOU. ACT
FOR YOURSELF.
FACE THE TRUTH.

KATHERINE MANSFIELD

Time is a great restorer, and changes surely the greatest sorrow into a pleasing memory.

Mary Seacole

I DON'T THINK
OF ALL THE MISERY,
BUT OF THE
BEAUTY THAT
STILL REMAINS.

Anne Frank

YOU MEAN
SO MUCH
MORE THAN
THE MILES
BETWEEN
US

FIND A ZEN SPACE
IN YOUR MIND, EVEN
IF IT'S JUST SINGING TO
YOURSELF. JUST PASS
THE TIME AND KEEP
A STEADY BREATH.

MARY COPELAND

WE ARE ALL BROTHERS AND SISTERS AND HUMAN BEINGS IN THE HUMAN RACE.

Marsha P. Johnson

Face your life,
Its pain, its pleasure,
Leave no path untaken

Neil Gaiman

OUR UNITY IS
OUR STRENGTH,
AND OUR DIVERSITY
IS OUR POWER.

KAMALA HARRIS

YOU'RE GOING TO BE OKAY

If you're interested in finding out more about our books, find us on Facebook at Summersdale Publishers and follow us on Twitter at @Summersdale.

www.summersdale.com